# Aspazia Otel Petrescu:
# *With Christ in Prison*

## Translation by Elena Gabor

With an Introduction and Notes by
Octavian Gabor

Title: With Christ in Prison
Translation by Elena Gabor
Translation of the book *"Cu Hristos in celula"* by Aspazia Otel
Petrescu, published by the Areopag Publishing House,
Bucharest, 2011.
Introduction and notes: Octavian Gabor
Contributing Editor: David Dulceany
Editor: Ioana L. Ene


ISBN: 978-1-936629-36-7

Printed in the United States of America

Published by Reflection Publishing
P.O. Box 2182, Citrus Heights, California 95611-2182
email: info@reflectionbooks.com
www.reflectionbooks.com

# Contents

## Note about this edition

This translation follows the volume *Cu Hristos in celula* published by Areopag Publishing House in Bucharest, 2011. The book is a compilation of interviews and presentations given by Aspazia Otel Petrescu.

# Birth-Givers of Beauty:
## An Excursion into Finding One's Given Place within a Constellation

Suffering is usually understood within a binary system, with perpetrators and victims. In Aspazia Otel Petrescu's *With Christ in Prison* the readers will indeed find innocent people who suffered at the hands of their torturers. They will be thus tempted to side with the victims, with the "good guys," and perhaps despise those who inflicted senseless suffering. Those who lived during communism, in Otel Petrescu's Romania or elsewhere, know that we always talked about them—an impersonal but powerful "them," because they influenced all aspects of our lives. They listened to everything you said; they brought potatoes at the grocery store; they could put you in prison; they could turn you over to the secret police; they were the secret police. They were the "bad guys." But somehow they were also us. And we were them. In fact, one perhaps surprising feature of many testimonies about the suffering during the communist persecution in Romania is that those who suffered do not accuse. They do not accept the evil brought by communism either, but they situate themselves in a completely different realm, one in which there is no longer a binary system, with good and bad people, but rather only one:

the world in which we all live and for which each and every one of us is primordially responsible. While it reveals the darkness and the evil that can, at moments, overwhelm a human heart, Aspazia Otel Petrescu's volume is a testimony to the beautiful of this world.

There are no good and bad people in Mrs. Otel Petrescu's book, but only people who were living in a world dominated by evil and who responded to it in their own ways. Some were completely overpowered and allowed evil to act through them. Others resisted with a strength that they found within themselves, but a strength that was not of their own making. All of them—and all of us—were the battleground on which the struggle between good and evil took place. Aleksandr Solzhenitsyn, survivor of the Soviet Gulag and acclaimed author of *The Gulag Archipelago*, captured this fight in these few, but powerful lines:

> Gradually it was disclosed to me that the line separating good and evil passes not through states, nor between classes, nor between political parties either—but right through every human heart—and through all human hearts. This line shifts. Inside us, it oscillates with the years. And even within hearts overwhelmed by evil, one small bridgehead of good is retained. And even in the

best of all hearts, there remains... an unuprooted small corner of evil.[1]

In *With Christ in Prison*, we can see as well that the fight against communism is not necessarily between them and us; instead, it becomes a fight against one's own corner of evil. It is a fight against de-personalization, against becoming merely a member of a group, them or us. But this is not surprising, since the danger present in any fight against evil is to see oneself, either alone or as the member of a group, as the source of the good. If one gets there, then one becomes righteous and unforgiving and is one step away from murdering in the name of the "good." However, in the depths of Otel Petrescu's words, we can discover that the fight begins with emptying oneself of one's own ego.

It is certainly relevant that communism sought the de-personalization of human beings. In its claim to be able to rebuild a human, to create a "new man," an ideal one, communism also claimed that a person can be fully defined if considered in itself, separate from any one around it, and being understood only in relation to the whole—to the communist state. As any totalitarian regime, communism broke people from their personal connections: family, friends, their ancestors, and even their offspring. The "new man" had to completely

---

[1] Aleksandr Solzhenitsyn. *The Gulag Archipelago.* Vol II. New York: Harper Perennial, 2007, p. 615.

wipe everything that came from the past, for the past was corrupted.[2] A new man is rebuilt completely, after everything that constitutes his belonging to the former world is revealed, unmasked, and denounced.[3] Communists shared this ideal with the fascists, although "officially" they were enemies.[4] This "new man" was utterly unconnected with anyone else, for the only ties allowed were those with the party-state. In fact, any totalitarian regime brings with itself separation between people and thus death. People are alive in their connections with others. Once these connections are lost, they are no longer persons, but individuals who can be commanded. They are no longer free participants in a living world, one in movement,

---

[2] Gabriel Liiceanu in his *Dragul meu turnator* (*My Dear Informant*), published at Humanitas in 2013, points to this feature of any revolution. He says, "The majority of social revolutions, beginning with the French one, transform the members of the revolutionary society into *prisoners of the present*. The past is demolished, and history begins again, with the 'year 0.' Nothing can remind them of the past" (p. 162, my translation).

[3] The Pitesti Phenomenon, probably the most horrific experiment during the communist persecution (see Dumitru Bacu's *The Anti-Humans: Student Reeducation in Romanian Prisons*. Englewood: Soldiers of the Cross, 1971; also, Virgil Ierunca's *Fenomenul Pitesti*. Bucuresti: Humanitas, 1990), aimed precisely at this reconstruction of man.

[4] In this context, the "friendship" between Hitler and Stalin at the beginning of WWII should not be surprising. Fascism and communism, while opposed on the surface, stem from the same hatred against personhood.

shaped by the connections of the people belonging to this world, but rather fixed objects that can be manipulated by the party according to its purposes, whatever these purposes may be. The violence against the young generation that took place in the late 1940s and early 1950s has at its base this desire of breaking the people by destroying the connections that existed between persons.

A totalitarian regime hates the given world composed of connections among people. It knows the "good" and thus redefines every person within it in accordance with this good. If any one does not fit the "ideal," that person is disposable. It is an "enemy of the people"—that is, of the "ideal world" as conceived by the totalitarian regime. In other words, the regime murders the already given beauty of the world that is formed in the relationships among free persons and recreates it to fit its "ideal." In her *The Origin of Totalitarianism*, Hannah Arendt emphasizes the fact that any such regime transforms a person into an object:

> Totalitarian movements are mass organizations of atomized, isolated individuals. Compared with all other parties and movements, their most conspicuous external characteristic is their demand for total, unrestricted, unconditional, and unalterable loyalty of the individual member... Such loyalty can be expected only from the completely isolated human being who, without any

other social ties to family, friends, comrades, or even mere acquaintances, derives his sense of having a place in the world only from his belonging to a movement, his membership to a party.[5]

Regardless of whether one succumbs and accepts the oppression of the regime, the status of any human being changes from that of the person, a human whose infinity is experienced in his or her relationships to other free beings, to that of an individual in the eyes of the party-state. The "followers" are "atomized, isolated individuals" who are potential enemies as long as they recover their personhood. Those who do not renounce their personhood, become an objectified group in itself, that of the objective enemies. Whoever is against this project becomes an objective enemy. It is no wonder that, when they came to power in Romania with the support of the Soviet army and then through falsified elections, [6] the communists created for themselves these

---

[5] Hannah Arendt, *The Origin of Totalitarianism*. San Diego: Harcourt, p. 323-4.

[6] The 1946 elections took place in a climate of hatred. The historical parties, the National Peasants' Party (Partidul National Taranesc) and the National Liberal Party (Partidul National Liberal) had huge difficulties in organizing rallies before the elections because of intimidation tactics. The communists also organized a fraudulent election that allowed them to form the government. According to the real results of the elections, the National Peasants' Party won the right

objective enemies: the enemies of the people. They could come from various social strata: wealthy peasants, students, intellectuals, priests, but usually were characterized by their freedom of thought. In any case, as Anne Applebaum says in her *Gulag: A History*, "people were arrested not for what they had done, but for who they were."[7] They were objects that did not fit the new order.

Father George Calciu, who spent 21 years in communist prisons, points to the transformation of persons into objects in one of his homilies to the youth, for which he suffered his second imprisonment.[8] He says, "Society considers you simply a component part, one brick lined up alongside other bricks. Your freedom in it is to function as a brick, fixed for all time. This freedom is the freedom of constraint, and in this lies your tragedy. For your true freedom lies within you, but you know

---

to form the government alone or through a coalition. The majority of its leaders as well as the leaders of PNL were imprisoned as political prisoners and died because of torture and miserable conditions.

[7] Anne Applebaum. *Gulag: A History*. New York: Anchor Books, 2003, p. xxxvi.

[8] Fr. Calciu was first arrested in 1948, when he was still a medical student, for his standing "against the introduction of Marxism and Bolshevism as the only philosophy taught in schools" (Father George Calciu, *Interviews, Homilies, and Talks*. Saint Herman of Alaska Brotherhood, 2010, p. 32). He was liberated in 1964, with the occasion of a general amnesty. In 1979 he was arrested a second time, after a series of seven homilies to the youth. He was liberated in 1984.

neither how to discover it in its true meaning, nor how to use it when at last you have found it."[9]

Aspazia Otel Petrescu's *With Christ in Prison* is a testimony for how one finds one's true freedom, how one remains a person. I refer here to only one aspect of her book for it brings with itself a beautiful concept: the fact that people are connected over centuries as in a constellation. Otel Petrescu talks about the power of the words of prayer because through them we enter into a connection with the people who came before us, the people who are contemporary with us, but also with those who have not yet come to be. She says, "In our prayers there were other people's prayers, other people who had probably been in similar situations, who prayed with the same words, who used those words to connect with the Divinity. The prayer's words allow me to be on the same 'frequency,' the same channel that connects me to God" (p. 26). If we take her words further, I think we can say that we are all connected in various constellations, the constellations that are themselves the beauty of the world. In a constellation every star has its own meaning. While it is a star, and in this sense the same as all the others, it has its own personal importance given by the responsibility it has for the whole. I call it personal for stars, in this framework, are persons, not individuals; stars are

---

[9] Fr. Calciu, *op. cit.*, p. 162.

fully understood in their beauty when we perceive them connected with other stars. In itself, a star is no different than any other star. There may be shades of brilliance, but there is nothing special about them in separation. They are just bricks, as Fr. Calciu described the people of a totalitarian regime. Personhood is gained through belonging to a body; stars are persons in their connectedness with other stars, for we discover them as what they are in their own constellations. Constellations show both the uniqueness and irreplaceability of every star, for there is no star in the sky that can take the place of another one. They also show that a star finds its personal being only in communion with the stars of its constellation. Otel Petrescu reminds us that constellations are formed not only with the people in our contemporary world, but also with those who came before us. The connections established in families are a proof for this. In a family, we see that we are not the source of these constellations (as communism and fascism erroneously think when they want to create the world as they want) but we are responsible for that which is already given to us.

Otel Petrescu's book shows us how ugliness comes into the world by the breaking of connections. On the one hand, the first crisis comes with the communist attack against families, against tradition, against the past. On the other hand, the second crisis can appear when the persecuted people refuse to see their torturers as persons. To refuse to accept another person in your heart is to refuse an already given constellation; it is the refuse to love your neighbor. We do not choose our neighbors: they are given to us. In this sense, the beauty of this world is already created for us; it is already present. For the neighbor is the face, to use a term consecrated by the French philosopher Emmanuel Levinas, that calls on you to acknowledge the presence of a constellation. Refusing the neighbor (who may happen to be your torturer) is refusing the participation in beauty; is accepting ugliness, separation, and, I may add, objectivity.

I mentioned above that when communism came in power it broke the constellations formed over time by "denouncing" the past. But they did not stop at rhetoric. Indeed, communism destroyed families. According to Fr. George Calciu, communism wanted to break the connection between generations. To do so, the communists took an entire generation of intellectuals, mostly students, the promise of the future, and put them in prison and tortured them. The purpose was either to transform them into followers of the party's ideals or to annihilate them. Separating people from their source, from their relationships with others, is provoking a break in constellations. No longer shining in community (within their family, nation, or humanity as a whole), being separated from the source, they completely disappear from the sky. The intention to create a "new man" was for all purposes the attempt to make human beings live as atomized, isolated individuals, as Hannah Arendt says. The victory of communism is manifested in the complete transformation of a person into an individual. The disappearance of communities (constellations) comes with this, for communism does not fight against personhood only, but by implication also against the beauty of the entire world.

Why make this distinction between a person and an individual? An individual is determined; it has clear properties that define it and make it the member of a group, identical in these properties with all of the other members. An individual is thus replaceable with another individual. This means that I cannot enter into a genuine, personal connection with an individual. Genuine communication with another human being is always surprising, always unexpected, because the other is an infinity of possibilities. This other is not an individual "clothed" with ideas that comes with his or her own ideologies and enters into dialogue with my ideologies. The other is not "the torturer" or "the victim." The other is a naked *person*, and in this nakedness we communicate and form constellations. The similarity between all of us is nakedness. It is in this nakedness that we find the realm within which the dialogue between people can be truly authentic.

Thus, in my nakedness, the only thing that I can do is *be* with the other. Being with the other is not respect; it is not agreement either; but it is love. It is telling the other: "I know that I am not me without you; I know that I am connected with you, and that I was connected prior to being aware of this connection; and I thank you, my brother, for also being with me; and forgive me for any suffering that you go through because I am already a part of it; I am responsible for it." In constellation, there is no *them* and *us*; there is only presence and communion: the already given beauty of the world.

Aspazia Otel Petrescu's volume uncovers the lack of connection and the ugliness that is brought in this absence. My responsibility is to be with my torturer in his brokenness, for if my brother is in hell, I am already there with him. And it is so that hell is transformed through our embrace and presence for one another into heaven. In this connection we are for ourselves and for the others birth–givers of beauty.

Before I end, allow me to bring to mind the parable of the prodigal son (Luke 11:11-32), and not because of the prodigal son, but rather because of the older brother. The older brother is upset when the father rejoices that his younger son returned. He believes that it is unjust to not make him suffer; for him, it is unjust to celebrate with a fattened calf and to put a ring on his finger and a new robe on him. Many of us, at a moment or other in our lives, feel like the older son. The older son does not want his brother to be in his constellation because the brother first broke all connection. But the brother has returned. And he has returned ready to acknowledge his sins. It is in this returning that he needs to be received with love, for through the love that he receives the light of his star may shine again.

The older brother does not realize that perceiving injustice holds unto brokenness by perceiving the other not as a person, but as an individual who does not have the properties that would make him worthy of being a member of a group. The older brother transforms his constellation to a private club that requires certain properties.

How, then, can one respond to injustice in the world? Perhaps by perceiving the other, any other, including the torturer, as a face, as a promise for holiness.[10] To see that both of us are attacked by the same fears and that violence is the source of this fear. To see the torturer as more wretched than I am and to perceive me as responsible for his wretchedness. Not responsible to save him or her by bringing him or her into *my* constellation, but rather responsible for the state of the world and for the lack of love that he receives (or that he is unable to receive). Giving from what you are means shining with your light so much that you give yourself to the whole constellation. A birth giver of beauty is responsible as person for the beauty of the entire constellation.

--------

[10] In an interview for the documentary *Beyond Torture: The Gulag of Pitesti Romania*, produced and directed by Alan Hartwick, Father Roman Braga says that we have to see in everyone a candidate to holiness.

In his *Beginning to Pray*, Anthony Bloom speaks of such birth-givers of beauty, but he calls them humble persons. He reminds us that humility comes from the Latin word *humus*, which means "fertile ground." He continues:

> To me, humility is not what we often make of it: the sheepish way of trying to imagine that we are the worst of all and trying to convince others that our artificial ways of behaving show that we are aware of that. Humility is the situation of the earth. The earth is always there, always taken for granted, never remembered, always trodden on by everyone, somewhere we cast and pour out all the refuse, all we don't need. It's there, silent and accepting everything and in a miraculous way making out of all the refuse new richness in spite of corruption, transforming corruption itself into a power of life and a new possibility of creativeness, open to the sunshine, open to the rain, ready to receive any seed we sow and capable of bringing thirtyfold, sixtyfold, a hundredfold out of every seed.[11]

This volume brings to you the testimony of such a birth-giver of beauty: Aspazia Otel Petrescu.

Octavian Gabor

---

[11] Anthony Bloom. *Beginning to Pray*. Paulist Press, 1970, p. 35.

# Aspazia Otel Petrescu's Biography[12]

Aspazia Otel Petrescu was born on December 9, 1923, in the village of Cotul Ostritei, in her maternal grandparents' house. She was the first child (followed by brother Anatolie) of teachers Ioan and Maria Otel. She attended primary school in Ghizdita (Fantanele). She started high school in Balti, but withdrew due to prolonged illness. Between 1936 and 1940 she attended the all-girls Elena Doamna High School in Cernauti (city in today's Ukraine). [13]

During the tumult of 1940 she missed another school year. The following year, she made up her schooling through private tutoring. On March 18, 1944 school was interrupted by war bombardments and Aspazia went into refuge in Transylvania. She finished high school at Orastie (city in south-western Transylvania, Romania), in 1944, under bombardment. Between 1944 and 1948 she attended the Babes Bolyai University in Cluj, in the Department of Literature and

---

[12] Aspazia Otel Petrescu's biography first appeared in *Rost*, no. 64, 2008 (note from the Romanian edition).

[13] Elena Doamna was the wife of Alexandru Ioan Cuza, the Romanian leader who accomplished the union between Moldova and Tara Romaneasca (Valahia) in 1859. Many Romanian high schools are named after her, even today. Cernauti is the main city in the historical province of Bukovina, part of Romania between the two world wars and annexed by the Soviet Union after WWII.

Philosophy. She spent freshman year in Sibiu where the University was taking refuge, and then finished the rest of her schooling in Cluj. She presented the paper *Jesus in Romanian Poetry* at the Romanian Orthodox Brotherhood conference.

She became one of the favorite students of poet and philosopher Lucian Blaga, who encouraged her to continue writing. In fact, the philosopher followed her career and inquired about her after she became a political prisoner. As coincidence would have it, Lucian Blaga was himself imprisoned by the communist regime, as were many of his "sacrificial generation" whose destinies oscillated between prison and anticommunist exile.

Between 1946 and 1948 she worked as a stenographer at the prestigious Center for Transylvanian Studies, led by academician and historian Silviu Dragomir. On July 9, 1948 she was arrested right in the middle of an exam. She would not get the chance to graduate. She was sentenced to 10 years in prison. She served her sentence in three different locations: Mislea, Dumbraveni, and Miercurea Ciuc.

The reason for her arrest was not an unusual one for the atheist communist regime of the time: while at the Elena Doamna High School in Cernauti, Aspazia had belonged to Cetatuia, the women's youth group of the Legionary Movement, similar to the Brotherhood of the Cross for men.

In 1958, instead of freedom, she was condemned to 4 more years in communist prisons. She served her sentence between 1958 and 1962 at Mislea, Jilava, Botosani, and finally Arad, where she gained her freedom. In 1958, after the death of her father, she lived in Roman (city in north-eastern Romania) with her retired mother. With great difficulty, she found a job as an accountant at a shop in Roman.

In 1964 she married widower Ilie Alexandru Petrescu and raised his two children. His son later became an engineer and his daughter became a medical doctor. Her mother died in 1977, her husband in 1987, and her brother in 1998. After the fall of communism in 1989, she participated in all public ceremonies honoring the martyrs of the communist prisons and co-organized the Holy Paraklesis of Mislea (inaugurated on November 12, 1994). In 2007 she received the *Lucian Blaga Foundation* Award for short prose at the Lucian Blaga International Festival in Lancram (Sebes, Deva).

She published the volumes: *I cried to you, O God* (Bucharest: Buna Vestire Publishing House, 2000), prefaced by Prof. Ion Coja and in collaboration with her friend in suffering, writer Gheorghe Stanescu; *The Cross of Miercurea Ciuc and the Paraklesis of the Birth of the Mother of God* (Bucharest: Scara Publishing House, 2001); *I remembered* (Roman: Rovimed Publishers). She is also working on a book of essays and articles in two parts: *In Memoriam* and *Wheat Heads*.

# With Christ in Prison...[14]

*Among my memories there was an image of Apocalypse. I was going with my grandpa to church, on Pascha. We were holding hands. On the other shore, at Mihailovka, I saw how the cross, the bells, and the belfry of a church were thrown in the river Nistru. It probably was the church from the village. Everything was happening in the noise of tractors. Then grandpa told us children the following words. I considered and I still consider them his political testament: "Watch, remember, and never forget what communism means!"*

(Aspazia Otel Petrescu)[15]

*Interviewer*: Mrs. Aspazia Otel Petrescu, what is the most important thing you wish to tell our generation concerning your experience in prisons?

*AOP*: This question is a huge one and the words to answer it escape me. I would not dare give advice to the next

---

[14] Interview conducted by Vasile Danion.

[15] The quote comes from "O viata in temnitele comuniste" ("A Life in Communist Prisons"), published in *Monitorul de Neamt*, March 17, 2007. It was also republished in *Rost*, no. 64/2008, issue dedicated to Mrs. Aspazia Otel Petrescu (note from the Romanian edition).

generation. I can only say that each generation has its mission. Our generation was challenged to sacrifice themselves in prisons. I think that the generation that follows us will have to bring our sacrifice to fruition. As much as possible, of course, especially because the generation I am addressing will be tested more than we were. The traps, if we can call them so, are many and perfidious; it is much more difficult to face them today.

We had one big thing before us: we had to resist the imposition of atheism, the communist apostasy; nothing more. Now, the apostasies are multiple, more comprehensive, more perfidious, more difficult to discern. Of course, the fight is very difficult from this point of view. If I were to give advice from my experience, the pillar that keeps you from faltering is our Savior, Jesus Christ. There are many philosophies; even theology offers many paths. But, in order to avoid making a mistake in this turmoil of ideas and manipulations, to call them what they are, one must always refer to the same pillar, the same example. We know that the Savior is the Way, the Truth, and the Life. Thus, any time you are in a situation in which you do not know which path to choose, the question you must ask is, where would the Savior advise me to go? Or where would the Savior lead me? Or, more clearly, what did the Savior say in a similar situation?

In prisons, we didn't have priests as cellmates, especially us women, of course... From this point of view, the men were luckier for they had among them high clergy and priests of great spiritual integrity. We were alone, more isolated. But you should know that any time we had a dilemma we always found the right answer, the answer that never deceived us, in the life and the teachings of our Savior, to the best of our understanding.

However, in order to obtain an answer and to be certain about it, you need to communicate with God in a certain way; you need to know how to ask. Jesus said, "Ask and it will be given to you, seek and you will find." You will find what you seek if you want to find it, you will know if you want to know. Prayer helps and supports this knowledge. Prayer is the most powerful weapon. On the one hand, prayer works through the words you pray. On the other hand, prayer works through your personal boldness and aspirations, expressed through the words you choose personally. Prayer comes on two levels. You achieve the first level through the words that have been already said and that have a tremendous value. In prisons, we realized the extraordinary value of the text of a prayer. You may say that the prayers come with old mentalities, with problems from another time; you may say that the words are old, that they come from a distant past, and that we are different now. This is not true. The whole experience of man's faith and prayer is deposited in words, in the text, from the beginning of humanity until now. Basically, there is a tremendous storage of spirituality. The one who helped me understand that words are alive and that they are aged and enriched by previous experiences and meanings was Fr. Arsenie Boca.[16] He spoke to people using living words. When he was asked a question, he would answer in very short sentences, without using theological theories. His sentences were short, but you could feel the living words. I'll give you an example. Someone asked him, "Father, we seem to live in a determinist era, where our lives are determined by so many things. Can we then truly speak of freedom here on earth?" Fr. Arsenie said, "Yes, there is one kind of freedom that is complete and absolute—the freedom from sin." Period. The entire Christian philosophy was comprised in his answer.

You are free in as much as you can free yourself from the sins that dominate you. Father Arsenie gave all the valences acquired throughout history to this word, "freedom," despite its complexity of meaning. And he spoke very simply. That is what prayer meant for us in prison. In our prayers there were other people's prayers, other people who had probably been in similar situations, who prayed with the same words, who used those words to connect with the Divinity. The prayer's words

---

[16] Considered by many the Saint of Transylvania (western region of Romania), Fr. Arsenie Boca was himself a victim of the communist regime. Mrs. Otel Petrescu first met Fr. Arsenie before her imprisonment.

allow me to be on the same "frequency", the same channel that connects me to God.

Today all of us Christians are called to be in Christ's army, to confess our faith; we cannot just contemplate the world around us in a *dolce far niente* state of mind. We are called to confess our beliefs with courage and determination. My advice for these soldiers of Christ would be to choose two or three short prayers they could remember in times of need. We, the Orthodox, have the well-known hesychastic prayer, Jesus' prayer: "Lord Jesus Christ, Son of God, have mercy on me a sinner." The prayer to the Mother of God told in hesychastic spirit is also very strong: "Holy Virgin, have mercy on me, a sinner," followed by, "Lord Jesus Christ, have mercy on me a sinner." A good Christian should be armed with these prayers that put him quickly and effectively in contact with the Divinity and lift his soul.

You don't have to know them by heart, as I mention in my memoir; in certain situations you don't even use prayer. This is why I titled my book, *Lord, I Have Cried Unto You*, because this is what I did. In a crisis situation I didn't think about using my prayers although I had my own. I just didn't have time. I simply cried, I cried with desperation, and God heard me. I was put in a pit full of rats. It was right after an investigation of a policewoman, Laszlo, one of our guards. We didn't care much about our guards; they were who they were and they represented what they represented. We didn't care about them, but we also didn't hate them. Laszlo was very tough and she gave severe punishments, but always within the rules. She never added to our penalties like others did. They did it for their personal benefit. She was not cruel. I was sent to solitary confinement three times because of her, and that was a lot, but I did not hold a grudge against her. We were touched when, during walks, Laszlo would tell us stories about her daughter Antonia. We liked the name Antonia; it had an Orthodox resonance, although this guard was Hungarian and Catholic or Protestant, I am not sure. So we were impressed by how much she loved her daughter and by the fact that she shared that love with us, "the bandits" —because that's what she knew about us, that we were some dangerous, murderous bandits from the mountains.[17] One of the women in our group, Oltea Manoliu, the president of the Orthodox Club in Iasi, who was a senior medical student when she was arrested, was also a very talented painter. She and I were similar in that we both got arrested right before graduating from college. I was a good tailor and designer, so we decided to make a dress for Antonia for her baptism, a little, cute dress with traditional motifs.

---

[17] The Communist propaganda pictured all opponents of the regime as "bandits" ready to engage in criminal acts bent on overthrowing the "democratic" regime.

*Interviewer*: She was baptizing her daughter despite the official atheism?

*AOP*: Yes. Both Hungarians and Romanians baptized their children, some in secret. I used to work with a woman who was the chair of the local communist party, and she took her children to be baptized without her husband's knowledge. Duplicity was the norm.

*Interviewer*: This duplicity was everywhere.

*AOP*: I guess you can say she was duplicitous just like everyone else. So, as I was saying, in prison we did needlepoint. Take a look at this icon; it was made in needlepoint.

*Interviewer*: And the colors?

*AOP*: Everything. We used thread from shredded cloths; we used everything we could get our hands on, because we didn't have much in prison. Having a needle was illegal. If you got caught with a needle, you could grow old in solitary confinement. Well, despite these obstacles, we made a dress for Antonia, with Snow White and the seven dwarves on it. Right in the middle of the skirt we drew Snow White and all around the skirt the seven dwarves, each with their representative craft, like in the story. It was a gorgeous dress. Well, Laszlo missed work the day we finished it, because she had been scheduled for vacation. But she wanted it, so she asked a colleague to get the dress out of the prison for her. The first colleague she asked could be trusted, but she said "no" and told her, "Don't you realize what you're getting yourself into by accepting this dress? If, God forbid, they seize it, it's going to be the end of the world, so please don't get me involved." The next person she asked had the worst character and was not trustworthy; nevertheless, she said "yes." This whole thing took place at the prison in Miercurea Ciuc. This guard had been transferred there for disciplinary reasons and was therefore boycotted by the others. She was from the South (Olt county) and her colleagues were all local Hungarians.[18] Antonia's mother felt pity for her and invited her to stay at her place. And you wouldn't believe it, but this creature figured she could put Laszlo in prison, stay in her house, get her husband and everything she had for herself. Laszlo's family was pretty well off, and her husband worked as a craftsman in a cooperative that was semi-private under communism and where people could make decent fortunes in the trade. So the guard came and got the dress we made for little Antonia, but instead of taking it to Laszlo, she took it straight to the authorities and told them that she found the dress during a cell inspection and the prisoner confessed making it for Laszlo to buy her goodwill, which was not true at all.

---

[18] In Miercurea Ciuc there is a large population of ethnic Hungarians.

I clearly remember that summer day; it was June-July, a beautiful day. We were just back from our walk. She came to us in the first cell, took Oltea aside so that we couldn't hear, and told her, "Give me the dress." "What dress?" "Stop pretending, you know what I'm talking about. Laszlo asked me to get the dress for her." Then Oltea came back to the cell and told us, "I don't know what to do." There were six of us in the cell. We thought about it and decided we should give it to her thinking that Laszlo trusted her. We also wanted to get rid of the dress because it was really hard to hide it during cell inspections that occurred every ten days. So she gave her the dress, and then hell broke loose. Everybody in prison started hating us for setting Laszlo up. They realized the dress had been our initiative, not Laszlo's, and they thought we tried to tempt her so to speak and then turned her in. A rumor started that she would resign during her vacation. She really wasn't fit to be a guard. Everybody hated and despised us.

At one point, the whole prison staff stormed into our cell: the assistant manager (we were lucky the general manager was on vacation because he was a brute—Romanian, unfortunately; the Hungarian assistant manager was more humane), the political officer, the shift supervisor, the prison lieutenant, the external security guard... The entire staff came into our cell. The room was full. They searched it high and low. They searched even underneath the wood floor. They put us all in isolation and left only the two older ladies—Mrs. Liliana Protopopescu and Lizica Papasterie, two key witnesses in the anti-legion trials going on at the time. Oltea Manoliu, Viorica Barnac, Sofica Cristescu, and I were placed in isolation in different cells throughout the prison so that we could not communicate or do anything. They had their plans and we had ours. The ones with the best plan would win. We had a lot of experience and they knew that we could find a way to avoid this whole thing, so they isolated us.

They took me to Isolation Room #3. There were four isolation rooms at Miercurea Ciuc in the basement. In the back of Isolation 3 there was a door, and we never knew what was behind it. I was the first one to find out. I wasn't there for long. The floor supervisor came. Her name was Erji, and we liked her character the most. She told me, "Hey, how could you do something so bad?" She barely spoke Romanian. "You wanted to make a dress for Antonia, you made this dress, Laszlo couldn't take it out herself, so she sent the other one instead, and you, instead of giving her the dress, you reported her up the chain, told a lie, and look now, Laszlo will be arrested and sentenced—very, very bad." I had an expression of shock on my face and I said, "Ms. Erji, this is not true!" I told her the truth. And she said: "Oh, bitch." She was the first to realize what had happened. "I see, she wanted to stay in Laszlo's home and have free reign. I will tell everyone the truth and the situation will change." She told me, "Everyone hates you. How could you do such a thing?" "We didn't, we just don't know how to get out of this now." I also told her, "Ms. Erji, I will pretend I don't know anything. But I need to know what Oltea will say so that we all say the same thing. I will wait for a Morse message through the wall or some kind of message telling me what to say. Till then, I will pretend I don't know anything. Just so you know."

She said, "I wouldn't do that if I were you. You know the proverb 'the shirt is closer to your skin than the vest.' Tell them everything you know, because you were not directly responsible anyway. In fact, Laszlo is very much afraid of you, because she put you in isolation three times, and she now thinks you did this to get revenge." And I said, "God forbid! I am telling you, I am willing to take a big risk to save her, not to get her in trouble."

And indeed they started investigating me. The General Manager of the prison questioned me with the dress on the table: "Tell us what happened."

I was cell leader and I was supposed to know everything that went on in my little cell. I said that I didn't know anything. But realistically it didn't make much sense because our cell was really small, one by two meters, with three bunker beds and very little space to move around. As room leader I was supposed to report everything suspicious or against the rules. So I played stupid and the manager lost his temper and said,

"I will put you in a place from where you will come out as black as this floor. I suggest between the two of us, that you should confess to everything you've done; just say you did it, you'll get your punishment and we'll move on. But don't make me get the truth out by force, because you'll spill it anyway. You've spent so many years here, you know there is no way out for you."

I told him, "Do whatever you want with me. I don't know anything." I played stupid.

He then called Erji and quietly gave her instructions. Erji took me to Isolation 3 where "Hitler" was awaiting. "Hitler" was one of the older employees at the prison. He was old and very, very mean. We called him Hitler not because he was mean, but because he resembled Hitler very much, had a little mustache, he was short in stature and had an awful character. He was mean in a special way. They had brought us new handcuffs, shiny, kind of beautiful, and we called them "American handcuffs". They locked using a rotation device, and they fit closely to the skin right at the wrist. Hitler never fitted them to your hands. Before these American handcuffs, they had used men's handcuffs on us, and we could get our hands out. We would put them back on when we heard guards coming. They knew about it. Then they brought new

"American" handcuffs, and Hitler cuffed me using his own method. He kneeled behind me and forced my hands to my back. Perhaps he was ordered to do that, because usually they cuffed us in front, so that we could eat or move our mattresses. With my hands at my back I couldn't do a thing. I felt the cuffs tightening on my wrists, and it hurt terribly. My nerves were pressed to a point of unbearable pain. When he saw my face cringe with pain, he left them on without setting the lock, which meant that with every move, the cuffs would get tighter and tighter on my wrists, close to the bone. If blood doesn't get to your hands for hours, you could lose your hands this way, and maybe this is what they wanted. I realized the manager had followed through on his threat, but I didn't say anything; I was paying for my silence.

Then he pushed me behind the mysterious door in Isolation 3. Poor Erji was looking at me with pity. Then she came to me and told me, "I can't help you. All I can do is tell others what you told me".

I told her, "You *can* help me. I trust you are trustworthy and understand my situation. Please go to Lazlo and ask her not to admit anything."

"But what should she say?"

"That she didn't know a thing, that she was completely ignorant of this. Even if they beat her during the investigation, she shouldn't say anything, if she wants to stay free and raise her daughter."

And Erji said, "I will not tell you anything because I don't know how strong you are."

She was being careful, knowing that under torture I might confess that I asked her to connect me with Laszlo and tell her to be silent. So prudently, she said:

"I won't tell you anything, I feel for you." And she left.

Then I looked around me. On the floor in front of the door shut behind me was a wooden platform. The room was in fact a very deep cellar with very little light. Behind the platform, there were some steps going down, and I could tell the cell was empty; the walls were black and wet. I looked around and wondered where I would sleep at night. I figured I would sleep on the wooden platform, but I was afraid of rolling down into the pit during sleep. Looking down I noticed some straws thrown here and there and I thought they could have at least given me a pile of dry straws for a bed in this humid cellar. However, when I looked closer, the straws moved. I saw shadows moving fast like arrows along the walls and towards the center. There were hundreds of rats crawling on the floor like dark moving shadows. I wondered, "Are they just mice or rats?" As if to confirm, one of them climbed up the stairs towards me. I remembered all the stories I knew about animals. I specifically remembered one saying that rats organize in groups led by a leader and that they fight as a group when attacked. One of them came to me and I thought, "This must be the leader of the group."

*Interviewer*: How big was it?

*AOP*: As big as a cat. It was big and well fed from the prison's reserves of grains. It stopped halfway and looked at me. I immediately thought, "They must be used to people." Usually rats avoid people, but this one stopped and looked at me. I had nightmares about that encounter for many months. Its eyes were small, without eyelids, and it had an empty stare. I thought Hell must feel like those eyes, emptied of all goodness and light.

*Interviewer*: Senseless.

*AOP*: Such an emptiness… An expressionless beast with no feelings… If I close my eyes, I see that infernal pair of eyes even now, and it gives me chills up my spine. It turned around probably thinking, "I'll deal with you later at night." You know, they say rats are pretty intelligent.

I didn't tell my cellmates the story of the rats when I came out. I told it to them long after 1989.[19] I didn't want them to know that there were so many rats in the prison; there were

---

[19] The communist regime fell in December 1989.

many sensitive people among us. Before that moment, I did not use to be afraid of mice and rats. Now I am afraid and repulsed. When I told the girls the story, they said,

"Your guardian angel told that rat not to move a step further."

Who knows? I was calculating how to position myself against the wall to protect my body, but with my hands at my back the front of my body was exposed. I couldn't push them away with my hands if they attacked me. The cuffs were getting deeper into my bone and my nerves were almost shot, so I couldn't move my hands at all. I said,

"God, I'm cornered. What do I do?"

I fell into a deep and dark despair. Very dark, I can't even describe it. I could see no way out. The only solution was probably to confess and do what the Assistant Manager anticipated when he put me in that room—to knock at the door and confess everything—which I could not do. I couldn't do it, because giving up would have meant to render all my previous suffering useless. I couldn't give up but I also saw no way out. I felt literally and practically cornered.

Then I thought, "I could just let myself fall down in the pit head first." But then I said, or rather my guardian angel said, "Hey, hey, that's a stupid idea." I realized what an idiot I was, because the platform I sat on was only ten feet off the floor, and there was no guarantee I could die, not even on a concrete floor.

I wasn't sure I would die, not even if I had thrown myself head first. And the rats would have made a feast out of me if they had sensed blood.

*Interviewer*: Didn't you think you'd commit a sin by killing yourself?

*AOP*: No, I was desperate, I was already in sin. Many priests told me afterwards, "You must have been in a special state of grace." And I told them,

"That's not true!"

Everyone should know that the more desperate and helpless you are, the faster the help comes from God. I was so desperate that I was ready to sin. In that moment I forgot to pray. I had spent eight years in prison by that time, so I was already a prisoner well versed in prayer. I was already in the mystical state of suffering. I had appropriated suffering in a transcendental way. But despite these spiritual accomplishments, I forgot them and sank in a dark despair. All I could see were the rats climbing on me and I was defenseless.

*Interviewer*: You were just thinking that, but they were not actually climbing on you, correct?

*AOP*: Correct. I was only feeling that way. And then I cried: "God, don't leave me!" I couldn't think of anything better or more intelligent to say to the Eternal Father. My desperation simply exploded out of me with complete sincerity: "God, don't leave me! You are my only salvation."

In that desperate situation, I realized that I was not cornered, that I had a door in front of me—the door to the Eternal Father. I can't stop tearing up when I remember the moment after that cry. It was a moment of grace that was bestowed upon me through the Eternal Father' mercy, not through my strength, because I had none. I only had desperation. I heard my own voice with what seemed like someone else's ears, the voice seemed different from my own. It was a strangled, raspy voice, it wasn't my usual voice, calm and pleasant, of which I used to be proud. When I said, "God, don't leave me..." the whole reality around me changed. There was no clerestory, no platform, no stairs going down, and no rats. There was nothing. There was only a big white light, and I was enveloped in it; I felt it as very concrete and material. It was a concrete, material light, and I was completely wrapped in it. I have never experienced a similar feeling in my life since then. The light was not like that from the sun or from a light bulb. It was a surreal light, how can I describe it? I've never seen something like that in my life. You know how sometimes in winter it snows with big snowflakes and then the sun makes the snow so bright and shining? That's how that light was—a vibrating, scintillating, amazing light. How can I describe it? I can't find the right words. I felt immersed in it and immensely happy—an overwhelming joy. It was like when you love someone with all your heart and you learn that you are loved back. That's when you feel a special joy and fulfillment, from giving and receiving love at the same time. I was living this feeling so intensely that, if it had lasted any longer, I would have turned into ashes. I was vibrating and scintillating in this joy and happiness. I didn't know what was going on with me, or that I was Aspazia Otel brought there by the guards. None of that. Just a vague knowledge of these things, a vague remembrance that I used to be a problem and now I was no longer one, that I used to be a dilemma and now I was no longer. I felt very happy to be out of all that and immersed in this light filled with love, joy, and salvation. I was filled with this overwhelming, indescribable emotion.

You could perhaps try to imagine it from my meager words. After a long period of time, the light left me and everything returned to normal. The rats were all lying down on the floor, no longer running left and right. There was a small clerestory in the shape of a half moon, and I could tell that it was getting dark outside.

I wondered: "God what will you do with me now?" However, I was no longer afraid, I was calm and relaxed, confident that the heavenly powers have not abandoned me, and that I will come out of this situation with a clean heart. I was very calm and centered. Still, I held onto the remains of that joyous, warm, maternal feeling that had wrapped my heart. I felt as safe and peaceful as a child at his mother's breast.

In the evening Erji came, opened the door, and said, "What I will tell you has to stay between us. I saw Laszlo and I told her everything; she said that if she were tortured she would think of Antonia, stay strong, and refuse to admit guilt." I told her: "Good." Earlier, before Erji's visit, I heard through the walls in Morse code ERLO. In Morse code it looked like that: dot, hyphen, dot, dot, dot, hyphen, dot, dot. After a while, I thought, "It must be Lena." Lena Constante was arrested for the Patrascanu trial.[20] It's true we had acted very nicely towards her and helped her in difficult circumstances, but we did not expect such gratitude from her—she was known to spread lies about the Legion. The Communist party spread all sorts of negative rumors about the Legion that will be believed by many for years to come, but we have remained untouched by them. Anyway, the fact the Lena talked about us in very negative terms after we had treated her nicely seemed pretty vile to me. At that time I had no idea she would have such an attitude, but we knew in what trial she was involved and what her worldview was, we knew all that, and I didn't trust her. So I did not reply promptly. I thought, "She can't be calling me."

---

[20] The readers can find Lena Constante's testimony in her book/memoir *The Silent Escape: Three Thousand Days in Romanian Prisons*. University of California Press.

And then I heard, "He is calling Pa." I was Pa—from Pazi, my call name. Then I tried to answer, but it was hard. I kicked an answer into the wall with my heel, but she kept "deleting" because she didn't understand. I was telling her, "Talk to me, I am in handcuffs, I can't talk." I ended with "talk, talk, talk" without other explanations, because I knew what she intercepted was only a partial message. In Romanian the word "handcuffs" uses special characters like "a" or "s" [sh], which don't exist in Morse. So what could she understand? As an anecdote, I will tell you a funny story. When we received "The Father's Letter" in prison, we received it in Morse code to learn it by heart and enjoy it as much as we could. The first line confused us tremendously. It said, "Son, oh, son, the road to you is long, over *big* ["mari"] and *strong* ["tari"]."

*Interviewer*: You mean "seas" ["mari"] and "countries" [tari"].[21]

*AOP*: Indeed. "Seas" and "countries". The special characters were missing in Morse code. That was Lena's problem too. So when she heard that all I said was "talk, talk, talk," she realized that I couldn't communicate much. My hands were tied at my back, I was kicking with my heel, and I

---

[21] In Romanian, the plural for "big" is "mari" and for "strong" is "tari." The Romanian word for "seas" is "mǎri" and for "countries" "țǎri".

didn't even have solid shoes, but soft shoes with cotton sole. It was hard work, a Sisyphus-like work to even say, "talk." She realized that she could not expect much from me and she told me the story.

The Samuel sisters, who were Jews and worked as secretaries at the American Embassy and English Embassy respectively, were frequently asked to answer questions in investigations related to arrests made at their embassies. They worked in key positions and were always called to testify. It is very likely that they were called again for an investigation, and they had recently heard about Nicola from Iasi, who had been released from prison, that she was now married and had a little girl. So we decided to come up with the following story: that Oltea decided to make a dress for Nicola's girl and send it through another prisoner, Viorica, our cellmate, who was about to be released in two weeks. Viorica was supposed to get the dress out of prison and take it to Nicola. I thought, "I was right to play dumb and not say anything to the interrogators. Now we can all say the same story and maybe we get lucky." Still, I knew that the situation was risky and in the hands of our guardian angels, because if the investigators would dig for details, we would be in trouble. The details could not be ironed out via Morse code through the wall. I said, "May God protect us from being asked for details. May the police accept our story as true." It was our word against Orlanda's word. We had nicknamed the traitor Orlanda; others called her the Yeller, because she was always yelling. All her colleagues spoke in negative terms about her, because Erji had told them the truth. After the prisoners of common law[22] learned that we were not to blame, one of them went and told the prosecutor from Bucharest. The local police said they were under-qualified to deal with the issue and asked for help from Bucharest. Luckily, they sent a young prosecutor, who was very, very smart and of good character, you'll see why. I'll tell you how he dealt with the case. Two days after the incident with the rats, I was taken in the interrogation room. I was still in the same state of grace in which the light had left me. One moment the light was there with me, the next it was gone.

*Interviewer*: How long did that state last?

*AOP*: Three days. I was interrogated on the third day. I was perfectly calm and very confident and grounded. When I said the story we had come up with, the prosecutor stood up (he thought he could dominate me through his tall, imposing stature). The other local interrogator sat down at the table. And I just thought of a little trick I could use, probably inspired by my guardian angel, because I usually am very direct and don't use tricks. But I used one then. Realizing the low educational

---

[22] While all political prisoners were usually kept separate, interactions with prisoners of common law sometimes took place.

level of the local security officer, I started speaking in the most elevated and radical way possible, using rarely used neologisms and jargon. I think the prosecutor had a playful spirit, because he answered in kind, and the poor local officer didn't understand a thing. The prosecutor said: "Ok, your story is very nice. Let's dissect it to see if the details work." And I thought, "That's exactly what I was afraid of."

He said, "Tell me, in what month and day did this incident happen? When did you hear from the Jewish sisters that Nicola has a girl and you decided to make a dress for her?" I said, "You're asking me to tell you when?" I spontaneously thought to say, "Mr. Prosecutor, you're asking the impossible. Those of us who have been in prison for a long time have lost track of time, we don't know what month or day we're in. We only know that it's summer, spring or winter. We lost track of days. We completely lost track of days. We'd need an extraordinary memory to remember the days." Of course, we had our methods to keep track of days, even if we didn't always know the exact date, we always knew Mondays, Wednesdays and Fridays because those were fasting days. We knew when the week would pass.

I was lying to the prosecutor, but we told ourselves that lies told during investigations would be forgiven. "I can't tell you what day it was." "Ok, at least approximate." "I can tell you what season it was. The acacias were in bloom." I thought the acacia stays in bloom for a long time and all the dates that other prisoners will give would fit within that period. He smiled, he realized what I was trying to do; he was smart; he said, "Oh, at least the chestnuts were not in bloom." There was a popular song at the time about blooming chestnut trees. I didn't smile; I pretended I didn't catch the irony. I saw him walking towards the window and then quickly towards me, and I thought, "watch out, he's going to slap me hard, off this chair." I thought he was going to hit me, but he only kicked my chair with his foot. I slid across the floor with my chair underneath me, and thought, "What got into him?" He seemed like a man with style, education, and good manners. Judging by the words he used he was smart and educated. He didn't seem to be a brute.

And he said, "Tell me what you, Legionaries, are made of. If someone would have done this to me, I would have jumped off my chair and swore at him, even hit him." And I said, "Well, you certainly realize I can't do that." "No, of course, you can't respond with a rude gesture to my rude gesture, but you could have blinked at least, which you didn't.

*Interviewer*: When he hit your chair, you didn't even blink?

*AOP*: Indeed, I realized in that moment that I didn't even blink. I thought, "Lord, great is your power!" Of course I didn't tell him any of that. I put my head down and he said, "So, what's your answer?" And I said, "If I answer you sincerely, you will not like it, you will not like it at all." "Well, let's try anyway." And I said, "In one sentence, we have a strong belief in God."

I was thanking God in those moments for keeping me unbreakable. I was in the mental state created by that miraculous light that got me out of desperation. It pulled me out of my reality and into another reality. Later, I realized that what had happened to me was, in theological terms, an experience of spiritual ecstasy. It takes you out of reality and carries you in a different world where there is light, happiness, and joy.

*Interviewer*: Have you had a similar experience since then?

*AOP*: Never. It was a unique event in my life. I had other dreams filled with light, but the light was ordinary. Going back to the story, the common prisoner came and stated,

"I had my parents pay this police woman [Orlanda] to connect me with my lawyer so that I could give her the key to getting out of the trial and it cost me this much."

That prisoner told on her and the prosecutor said:

"You just want to get revenge on her because she did something to you or she refused to do you a favor, and now you're lying to get her into trouble."

But the prisoner said,

"I am not lying. Just go to my parents, or call them and ask them if indeed they were visited by this person so and so, who brought this letter on this day, so and so."

I am not sure whether the prosecutor checked all these facts, but in any case she was now discredited as a policewoman and everything she said could be questioned and everything we said could be true or credible.

When I returned to my cell, Oltea said,

"Pazi, could you tell where this prosecutor was on the issue?"

I said, "As much as my state of mind and the questions allowed me to." She said, "I think he knew exactly how things were, or he really liked how we made the situation plausible, that he decided to take the story as it was." And I said, "What are you relying on when you say that?" She said, "You know what he told me?" "No." "He didn't interrogate me in the typical way." (For the typical interrogation the interrogator would ask a question written ahead of time and you'd give an answer that he would write down as he saw fit. You would answer in your own words, but he would use his own words that he would then read to you. If you agreed with what he had written, you'd both sign after every answer to eliminate any doubt of interference in the investigation.)

Oltea continues, "And he told me: 'I won't interrogate you in the typical way, I will let you write your own statement. Just be careful how you write it so that it resists the test of truth.' What do you think of that? He clearly said: 'Write it in such a way that it would be believable by anyone who reads it.'"

*Interviewer*: Do you remember the name of that prosecutor?
*AOP*: No, I never knew it.

*Interviewer*: How old was he?
*AOP*: About thirty. He was young, from the new generation of prosecutors. He was different from the ones who got your statements with torture. He asked subtle questions.

*Interviewer*: He might still be alive since he was younger than you.
*AOP*: Yes, he might. If he reads this book somewhere, he must be amused.

(During this interview, several young people were present. One of them, Marian Maricaru, asked): When you mentioned God to this prosecutor, what was his reaction?
*AOP*: When I told him that we believed in God he said, "Eh, these are bedtime stories." He couldn't say anything different because the other investigator was present.

*Interviewer*: What other difficult moments in prison do you remember?

*AOP*: The most difficult moment of the whole period was when I found out that after ten years of prison, of really hard prison, they gave me four more years. Not four years of administrative stuff they typically gave, but hard prison time. I knew they were not going to release me, since I had had tough trials. Diri's trial didn't take place anymore. Diri was the Mislea prison director. We called her Diri. The civilian prisoners called her "Diri neni," but we got rid of the Hungarian appellative "neni" and called her "Diri." Her real name was Elena Tudor, but we all remembered her as Diri. She was supposed to have a tough trial but it ended well. We are certain that it ended well because the whole prison, with the exception of the informers,[23] fasted and prayed for three days for the trial not to take place. And it did not, because the whole group in the Internal Affairs Ministry who were enemies of Diri fell—Chisinevschi, Teohari Georgescu, and the rest. They had to take the fall for Diri so that Diri would be saved, and she was. That was a difficult moment too. She was a very controversial person. She could be a beast, but she could also be very generous and crazily

---

[23] The informers were a common recurrence in political prisons. The inmates were either promised to be treated better (better portions of food, for example) or were cooperating with the administration on their own accord. According to Ion Ioanid's *Inchisoarea noastra cea de toate zilele* (*Our Daily Prison*), once they were known as informants, these people could not shake off their bad fame and were avoided by all other prisoners, even when they were sent to other prisons.

courageous. Few of us could have saved as many lives as she did, as bravely as she did.

*Interviewer*: And how do you explain that double personality of hers?

*AOP*: In the beginning she was a true believer in communism, one of the intellectuals who believed in the *Communist Manifesto*, which sounds good when you read it first. Slowly, she realized what communism was, what bolshevism was, what this demonic intersection of pan-Slavism and New-Age-ism was. She realized what these things were and she felt deceived. The most interesting conversation I've ever had in prison was with her. At first, she treated us students very badly. She treated us badly because she was intrigued: why are the intellectual youth in prison? And she blamed us. In fact, we were guilty of not loving the communists, that's what it was! We didn't love them and they punished us for that, to put it simply...[24]

---

[24] (Note in the Romanian edition). In a radio testimony for *Radio Romania Cultural* on February 24th, 2011, Mrs. Aspazia Otel Petrescu gave further details about her extraordinary experience in the rat cell:

*... a terrible fear overwhelmed me, a horror so strong, that I involuntarily cried: "God, don't leave me!" I heard my voice and it scared me. It was raspy and strange, and I couldn't recognize it, my own voice. But in that moment when I cried, in a microsecond, everything around me disappeared: the cell, the rats, the steps—there was nothing, nothing of the*

*reality I had entered. There was an infinite light around me, but not the usual light of the sun or electrical bulbs. The light was... how can I say this... a material, concrete, palpable light. I was immersed in it, like I was swimming in it. It had a brilliant whiteness. I could compare it with the fresh snow shining under the sun, with thousands of sparkles. It was a gentle and beautiful light, and I felt so happy; I really cannot express that feeling of peace and plenitude. And I said: "God, I wish I could always remain in this new reality!" I did not really know what was going on. I just had a vague idea that I had a problem before and now it was gone. Just that, at one point, this experience became so intense that my poor soul, unworthy of such a gift, was burning and getting consumed with happiness if you can understand this paradox. However, I felt that I could not stand that overwhelming happiness, that I would be dissolved, consumed by it. I was unworthy and too small for such a great joy.*

*And from that moment on all my problems were solved. Everything ended the way we wanted it, including the investigation. I think God had mercy on me not just because of my cry, which was sincere, from the bottom of my heart, but I also think the prayers of the other women mattered, as the whole prison knew about the investigation and everyone in prison prayed for me. I cannot find the words to tell you how wonderful that feeling of communion and togetherness was when, at a signal, the whole prison said the thanking prayer.*

# Prayer Saved My Life[25]

*Interviewer*: How do you see the prison period now?

*AOP*: I consider it an honor, just like Petre Tutea[26]. I am getting emotional now ... [tearing up] ... we all do when we think of the great honor that God granted us when He placed us on the same lineage opened by Jesus Christ the Savior. We answered a call to suffering that was supposed to wash the sins of our people and place it on an ascending path to salvation. Because the ultimate goal of a people, like for an individual, is not pleasure and earthly happiness, power and shiny temptations, but the Resurrection. God called on us to show that we are capable to sacrifice the most pure and beautiful years of our lives for the Resurrection.

*Interviewer*: St. Paul says that love came before everything. What did love look like in prison?

*AOP*: For us love was in the small things. A dandelion that you would bring from your walk for someone's birthday meant

---

[25] This is an excerpt from an interview recorded by Raluca Tanaseanu for *The Orthodox Family* magazine, issue 5, 2010.

[26] Petre Tutea (1902-1991) was a Romanian philosopher imprisoned by the communist regime between 1949-1953 and again between 1956-1964.

a whole garden especially that it was brought in with great risk and sacrifices. If you saw someone trembling in the cold, you'd go and hug her and warm her in your arms. Small gestures like these that you never forget. Our friendship is indestructible precisely because we were apprentices who wanted to learn the science to avoid antipathy, indifference, and separation from our neighbor, and replace it with tenderness, care, and love manifested in small gestures that appear huge when contrasted with apathy. We were not indifferent to our circumstance. The feeling of one was everyone's feeling. If one of us was put in isolation, we all suffered for her. We thought, "Poor her, she must be really cold and hungry..."

*Interviewer*: And of course, you prayed for each other. Please tell us about the wonders received in prayer.

*AOP*: Prayer saved my life. At one time I suffered from tuberculosis in both lungs. I had a fever, but I ignored it. I found out I had tuberculosis only after I got well. It happened while I was the head of the traditional seamstress workshop. I had an order from the Army Choir: 300 costumes for men and women, from seven different historical regions, plus white embroideries for their decorations. It was a tough order. We worked day and night. The order was placed in the spring and it was due on December 14th. It was already autumn, the days were shorter, we could not work many hours into the evening without electricity. I told the commander that we might not finish the embroideries. The costumes were ready, but the embroideries were not. The commander threatened me that he would write me down for sabotage because you "don't play games with the Army!"

I didn't say anything to the girls because I didn't want to force them to work in dim lighting. I said to myself, "He will write me down for sabotage and he'll lengthen my sentence. With the years I've already done, what's a few more?" But the girls learned from the production manager, a young woman hired by the Ministry to supervise production. The girls brought the embroideries to their rooms and worked on the upper beds where they had more light. They would work all night, and that's how the order was ready on December 14th. On December 9th it was my birthday. I had to tailor materials and calculate how much textile material was consumed. I worked 16 hours a day and didn't see the girls much. But every once in a while, I participated in the common prayers. After the Akatist, we said prayers for people who had special problems. And I could hear them say, "God, please give her strength, help her and free her!" And I would say after them, "God, please give her strength, help her and free her!" I didn't know that the prayer was for me.

On December 9th, they had a small celebration in the cell. On the table there was the famous cake made out of dry bread, gathered months in advance, and dipped in syrup obtained from medicine or marmalade obtained from the girls with special diets for TBC patients. Next to the small cake there was a card embroidered by hand—"Spiritual bouquet." The pages were made of cotton, and one could see how many prayers they had said for me from the wear on the letters made of thread. I was blown away by how many "Birthgiver of God" and "Our Father" had been said for my health. I had no idea I had TBC, but those who were doctors around me knew. They did not tell me to keep my morale up. The prayers of my friends healed me. When they brought X-ray machines to detect the TBC cases, I showed the sequels, which I still have today. The doctors wondered at how spectacularly I recovered. One doctor told me that I had a serious problem on both lungs, but you could barely see the signs. I told him I am forever healed. "But how can you be so sure, because the Koch bacillus can become active anytime!" I told him: "I didn't recover with drugs, I recovered with my friends' prayers—and what is healed from above stays healed!"

*Interviewer*: Is today's generation willing to sacrifice?

*AOP*: I live behind a public school. The words I hear coming out of the children's mouths today and their behaviors horrify me: "God, where will we be?" But I've also seen them crowding around the priest who teaches the religion classes. All the children wanted to be close to him. This man knew how to hold their souls in his hand. This is what we're missing—the educator, the role-model. Their souls are confused, the curriculum is planned in such a way as to be confusing and chaotic. They want the destruction of certain values, and they succeed as long as there is no element that could coagulate what is deep inside in the soul of a child.

*Interviewer*: What is the role of the parents?

*AOP*: It is primordial. It's not for nothing that we Romanians talk about "having seven years of education at home." But if the parents are not ready, if the parent was a bully himself as a child, he cannot educate his own. We need providential characters to create a special atmosphere in the parents' world and in the children's world. I don't lose hope. There are people out there who have not lost their way, who can walk the narrow path. I think that the generation who will be called to sacrifice for the salvation of our people will have to pass a much more difficult test than we did. We were destroyed with physical brutality, but this generation is destroyed with sweet temptations! Our children will have to do things they would not otherwise do, just to avoid the consequences.

*Interviewer*: Were there moments when it was difficult for you to forgive?

*AOP*: At the Botosani prison I was beaten once because I was the head of my cell and presumably because they found our cell to be messy one day. The pain was terrible. Week after week, the female guards would come to the bathroom to look at the scars on my back. The guy who beat me used a wide and long belt. He'd lift it up in the air and would hit me with all his might. He beat even two of my cellmates who spoke in my defense: "Why are you beating her up? Beat the ones whose beds were undone!" They were the prettiest ones, and I felt he wanted to ruin their beauty this way. As for me, when the pain got bad, I couldn't scream and I couldn't cry. That's how I am. This made the beaters even angrier though, because they thought I was defiant. I felt the pain, all right, but the pain silenced me. One time, this horrible beater bent down to see how I was doing and he saw my face grimacing with pain, and his face lit up. Just seeing the satisfaction on his face made me hate him. That was the only time in my life when I felt hatred. I actually got scared of that feeling, I realized that hatred is destructive, so I fasted for 40 days and ate only in the evenings to forgive him.

*Interviewer*: And did you?

*AOP*: Yes, I forgave him, but only after praying intensely. Seeing how hard I was trying, my friends helped me. I will not forget Eugenia Fuica. In order to help me get over my hatred and to make me think of the beauty of Christian love, she taught me "The Angel Cried" in a psaltic style that I liked very much. She did this when they took us out for our walk and they couldn't hear us sing.

*Interviewer*: You suffered a great deal. How can we accept suffering?

*AOP*: Suffering must be transfigured. Suffering can be transfigured through acceptance. One must find a reason for suffering. When you find the reason for suffering you are saved, because you can accept it. From that moment on, suffering becomes a joy, an honor. You realize that Jesus took a spoonful of His suffering and He gave it to you, your own cross. He won't have to carry it on his back anymore, it is up to you to carry it. So you become happy to be God's son.

# Lord, Hear My Prayer[27]

The first night was hard to bear, especially because of the acute cold and hunger. The hours from shut down to ten o'clock passed so slowly that I felt outside of time. But what terrified me the most were the small feet I felt passing over me shortly after laying down on the mattress. I thanked God for being forced to sleep with the light on. The dark would have amplified my terror. I tightly closed my eyes and refused to look at who was walking over me. Were they rats? Mice? I didn't want to know. I worked really hard at thinking it was all in my imagination. I was focusing so hard that I felt a cold sweat going down my spine. I decided not to get up because my feet were swollen and my skin stung, stretched over the frozen wood. I could not sleep. I tried to create a wonderful space in my mind, an escape into the sublime through imagination, but my tired mind refused to obey. Finally, I brought myself to Jesus' feet. I imagined seeking Him, finding Him and speaking to Him:

---

[27] (Note in the Romanian edition). The following is Aspazia Otel Petrescu's testimony about an experience lived in the Miercurea-Ciuc prison, as described by her in the book *Lord, I Have Cried unto You,* (Bucharest: Fundatia Culturala Buna Vestire, 2000, p. 310-312). The title we have chosen is the continuation of the prayer, "Lord, I have Cried unto You."

"Dear God, I know that somewhere in its core, even this prison has a heart. A narrow, cold heart like a prison cell where, after being dressed in insult and disgrace, they let you lay there hungry for truth and thirsty for love. You allowed yourself to suffer with us to lighten our burden.

"Tonight I was deeply wounded in my soul: I thought of all the wounds I caused You. Here I find myself among rats and cockroaches. These walls are hungry for my life. They absorb my body heat; I am hungry and cold, and I need your help. With You by my side, I am different from how *they* want me to be. But you are locked up, God, and I do not dare to step into Your prison cell.

"I prayed hard to not be caught by guardians, and I crawled on my knees all the way to Your door. I brought You two gifts for the wounds I caused You. I brought You the vigil candle of my soul. It is meager and ugly, because I have little gold in my soul and my craftwork is poor. But I crafted this light on the anvil of pain and in the flames of suffering, that is why I know You can increase its value.

"The light in this candle is as small as a poppy seed, because the oil that nourishes the faith is only a drop. A drop is all I could squeeze out of the seeds of my good deeds. Please God, multiply it like the wine at the wedding at Cana, or the bread in the desert. And thus, lightened up by You, allow the candle of my heart to illuminate the darkest corner of the prison cell, for the wounds I caused You.

"I brought you the flower of my heart. It is just a thin basil thread grown with difficulty. Its roots could barely grow on the stone of my heart. I watered it with my bitter, salty tears. But it grew and blew out of the miracle of Your love. Please receive this thread of basil, God, to flavor Your cell spiritually, in compensation for the wounds I caused You. I thank You, God, from the bottom of my heart, that you gave me communion with suffering."

And suddenly, the light in the isolation room became more calming and comforting. The cell seemed to smell like basil, and a pleasant warmth enveloped me, and somebody was speaking to me without words. I cannot explain it, but I could hear the words in my mind and in my heart: "Is there a desolate heart in here? Open the door, I am your friend, my name is Jesus." Then sleep came over me and I sunk in it with the same imponderability brought by feverish states.

# About the canonization of the saints who died in communist prisons[28]

*During a radio show Aspazia Otel Petrescu was asked: "Do you think that the believers who died in the communist prisons should be canonized?" Mrs. Aspazia Otel Petrescu answered:*

I will tell you one thing: in my limited view, there are two aspects that need to be considered. The first is that canonization is from the people, it is from their hearts, it is like a gratitude for the total self-sacrifice of this nation's saints and martyrs. However, for the heroes themselves, canonization doesn't mean much because they've already been judged up there. They "gave their report" up there, and they passed or not.

They are saints irrespective of our will, irrespective of our decision to canonize them or not. You should not believe that the Brancoveanus[29] were lesser saints because they had to wait for official recognition for such a long time. The people have

---

28 This interview was broadcasted on February 24, 2011 on the show "Creators of the sacred and the profane" on Cultural Romania Radio.
29 Here Mrs. Otel Petrescu is referring to Constantin Brancoveanu (1654-1714), Prince of Wallachia, who was forced to witness the beheadings of his four sons by the Ottomans before being executed himself. According to the Romanian Orthodox Church, the reason for his and his son's executions was their refusal to give up their Christian faith and convert to Islam. In 1992, the Church declared Constantin Brancoveanu and his four sons saints and martyrs. Their feast day is August 16.

recognized them as saints for a long time, even from the beginning. All the stories mention him as "a Romanian prince, a Christian prince." They have been saints all this time, even if the Church took a long time to make their sainthood official.

## Speech given at the blessing of the cross
## at Miercurea Ciuc[30]

Dear Holy Priests, audience, and sisters in suffering,

On behalf of the organizers, I welcome you here at the feet of this holy cross, built for the commemoration of our sisters who fell asleep during their years of detention, and who are buried all over the country in anonymous tombs without crosses. Let us unite our souls, those who could be here today with those who could not be here, but who are connected to us through the same grandiose dream shaped like our country for which we suffered. Let us thank the Good God for allowing us to commemorate the souls of the dead according to our Christian tradition at this good hour of our becoming, even if they died without a burning candle and without a loving hand to close their eyes, in the dark of the communist prisons; let us invoke their souls to join us in the battalion that God assigned to climb the Golgotha of prisons.

Come then from the skies and join us in waves of pure light to pray together one more time for the redemption of this people. Come to us from the earth in waves of water, to let our teardrops join the river of tears that wash the land of this country and the sorrow of this people. Come to us from the

---

[30] (Note in the Romanian edition). From *Lord, I Have Cried unto You*, (Bucharest: Fundatia Culturala Buna Vestire, 2000, p. 310-312).

past, from the catacombs of memory, to sing hymns of praise for the sacrifices made everywhere in the country for the resurrection of this people. Come to us from the future, in waves of spiritual incense, to burn together in the infinite love of the cross, love of country and of people. Come to us, you happy ones who took leave from this world that rolls in hatred, you who managed to dive in the divine infinity washed by tears; and because we are certainly together, let us offer us to God in one voice, one single heartbeat, in solidarity, strong and sublime. Let our heartbeat ring like a giant bell in all of His heavens to glorify His name, extolled in our tears, our sufferings, our crushed bones, and our own ashes.

Let us all remember how we could hear the bells from the neighboring church ring in our cells at the prison in Miercurea Ciuc. Let us give thanks to God for not deafening our hearts. We have no words to tell ourselves. We understand each other deeply and completely in silence. Words, regardless of their number or how well-crafted they are, cannot accurately translate crucifixions. We know how we were ripped by wild animals, how our hopes were stabbed, how our dreams were shattered, how we felt our way through swamps of desperation, how our knees bled during the helpless climbs on mountains of suffering, how our loves died, resurged, and died again drowned in tears and pain, how we fell, how we rose and fell again beyond the edges of human limitations.

They wanted to turn our bodies into stones for their temple, the so-called "best and most just world" that they built through unimaginable atrocities. Our bodies, our lives, and these nameless tombs bear the truths that must be confessed about a philosophy of life that believes in merciless crushing. Read in us, read us, dear people, and enlighten yourselves.

Those whom we deplore today have left us a long time ago, while those of us here are stepping into the sunset. The night is getting close for us too. The day is almost over, but all of us can find comfort in the fact that we didn't accept the communist "heaven" that invited us in through torture and terror.

We made another choice and this choice defines us as political prisoners. Instead of "merciless crushing" we chose "loving one another." This choice brought us light in the darkest nights and transformed us from prey into victors. In all prisons we have been through, we knew about the existence of the isolation cells, narrow and cold, where Jesus dwelled, dressed like us in clothes of shame and disgrace, sentenced to hunger for truth and thirst for love, just like us. Everything they did to us, He endured as well. Furthermore, he endured the wounds we gave him through our vanities, our quarrels, and our limitations. Oh, our guardians had no idea how He revealed Himself to us in secret as the God of love and compassion. He, the only One, was the author of this love, and we, poor hunted souls, were His sisters, along with His Holy Mother, His saints and His angels. We came together in Christ through love, and the closer we were to Him, the closer we were to one another. He was the Center and we formed a circle around Him, and the rays of His love warmed us all equally.

Through prayer we managed to bring discipline to the asceticism that was being imposed on us, and we learned slowly to conquer and in rare moments even to transcend what our torturers called our "miserable reality": cold, hunger, thirst, filth, terror, exhaustion, contempt, injustice, humiliation, and all the satanic range of sadistic compulsions.

Behind us we had a mountain of barbarism and indifference, ahead of us we had a gloomy, hopeless horizon, and the present was a slow, exhausting extermination. But we learned to bring fragments of time in the present that we could experience as happiness such that their light could fill the void created by the seemingly infinite intolerance and indifference. Let us thank God that love conquered all our limitations.

Most of us had no political ambitions and no philosophical dreams, but we had political poise. We were concerned with everything spiritually important, we had mentors and ingenious means of physical and moral survival. We did not crave the glory of the world, and not even the glory of the heavens, because our glory and heavens were where God was. That was our political stance. That is why they were merciless.

In prisons, we learned that the ministry to your fellow or to your country is done with personal and voluntary sacrifice, out of love. Our sisters who passed away learned this truth in the middle of the hatred that was unleashed against them. Not all of them had resounding lives; they lived simply where God placed them and gave them a certain road to take. They took that road all the way till the end. The lives of some of them were meager, some of them didn't live to be young, and those who did, lost it in prison. They chose the good side because of the generosity of their hearts, not because somebody imposed it on them. It was not easy for them to navigate the road to the great passing. No animal could bear so many wounds and unhappiness, but they endured them and carried their own cross - a cross that was huge, even if for some it may appear small, the size of a straw.

Today, here, for the rest of our lives, let us remain united and let us believe that all this effort was not for nothing. Everything came together, our legacy will grow in size, and the straw will support the future. We hope in the victory of our loved ones who have fallen asleep, because only through hope can we reach what is beyond hope. We hope in their victory because the God in whom we believe is the thrill of love and the gentleness of tears. He is just and keeps His promises. God cherishes the death of the devout and of the martyrs and He doesn't hide His tears.

With your permission, allow me to share the blessing of Father Ioan of Vladimiresti, Mother Mihaela's confessor. Mother Mihaela died in the horrible prison of Miercurea Ciuc. With pain in his heart he asked her to pray for Virgin Mary's intercession to heal the tragedy happening in our country and in her monastery:

"Bless, o God, the souls of Thy dead, and forgive their trespasses, both voluntary and involuntary, and grant them Thy kingdom and the communion with Thy Eucharist, Your endless love and the good life. Amen!"